E242
EDUCATION: A SECOND-LEVEL

LEARNING FOR ALL

UNIT 14
POWER IN THE SYSTEM

Prepared for the course team by
Patricia Potts

E242 COURSE READERS

There are two course readers associated with E242; they are:
BOOTH, T., SWANN, W., MASTERTON, M. and POTTS, P. (eds) (1992) *Learning for All 1: curricula for diversity in education*, London, Routledge (**Reader 1**).

BOOTH, T., SWANN, W., MASTERTON, M. and POTTS, P. (eds) (1992) *Learning for All 2: policies for diversity in education*, London, Routledge (**Reader 2**).

TELEVISION PROGRAMMES AND AUDIO-CASSETTES

There are eight TV programmes and three audio-cassettes associated with E242. They are closely integrated into the unit texts and there are no separate TV or cassette notes. However, further information about them may be obtained by writing to Open University Educational Enterprises Ltd, 12 Cofferidge Close, Stony Stratford, Milton Keynes MK11 1BY.

Cover illustration shows a detail from 'Midsummer Common' by Dorothy Bordass.

The Open University, Walton Hall, Milton Keynes MK7 6AA

First published 1992

Copyright © 1992 The Open University

All rights reserved. No part of this publication may be reproduced, stored in a retrieval system or transmitted, in any form or by any means, without written permission from the publisher or a licence from the Copyright Licensing Agency Limited. Details of such licences (for reprographic reproduction) may be obtained from the Copyright Licensing Agency Ltd, 90 Tottenham Court Road, London W1P 9HE.

Designed by the Graphic Design Group of The Open University

Typeset by The Open University

Printed in Scotland by Thomson Litho Ltd, East Kilbride

ISBN 0 7492 6114 5

This unit forms part of an Open University course; the complete list of units is printed at the end of this book. If you have not enrolled on the course and would like to buy this or other Open University material, please write to Open University Educational Enterprises Ltd, 12 Cofferidge Close, Stony Stratford MK11 1BY, United Kingdom. If you wish to enquire about enrolling as an Open University student, please write to the Admissions Office, The Open University, PO Box 48, Walton Hall, Milton Keynes MK7 6AB, United Kingdom.

CONTENTS

1	**Introduction**	4
	Studying this unit	6
2	**Changing power-relationships in education: a background for the 1990s**	7
	A Conservative cultural revolution?	9
	Labour's proposals: *Good Education for All*	11
	Putting Pupils First: the English Liberal Democrats	12
	Contrasting perspectives	13
3	**Losing ground and gaining ground?**	17
	Local education authorities	17
	Her Majesty's Inspectorate	18
	The perspective of a teaching union	19
	The National Curriculum Council	21
	Consumers	23
	Parent-power?	23
	Headteachers and school governors	23
	Voluntary organizations: developing a role in policy-making	24
	Conclusion: where does this leave parents and children?	26
4	**The politics of disability**	27
	Disability and oppression	27
	Care in the community: citizens or clients?	30
	Devalued identities	32
	Disability and charity	34
	Disability and political reform	37
5	**Conclusion: finding your way around the system**	39
6	**Investigations**	40
	What do school governors do? What powers do they have?	40
	'Beauty and the Beast'	41
	Independent living	42
	References	42
	Acknowledgements	44

1 INTRODUCTION

1.1 So far in the course you have read about those who, by and large, do not enjoy power in the education system: children and young people in schools and colleges who are devalued or excluded on the grounds of ability, disability, race, class or gender; their parents; classroom teachers; non-teaching staff. Among these groups are some whose power is supposed to be increasing: parents and school governors. Through the exercise of informed choice and the duties of lay governors, these consumers are said to be able to shape the education market of the 1990s – that is the rhetoric of the Conservative's 'Citizen's Charter'. This unit explores how far these proposed changes in the balance of power in education seem likely to be realized.

1.2 Those who have power have control over decision-making, channels of information and the allocation of resources. This unit aims to provide you with examples of the way in which power is exercised within the education system. I shall encourage you to compare the material in the unit with your own experiences within the education system, whatever your perspective.

1.3 What are the elements of the education system in the United Kingdom and what power do they have in relation to each other? Figure 1 indicates the elements of the state education system in England and Wales with particular legal powers and duties: central government, local education authorities (LEAs), schools under the direction of a headteacher, parents and governors. The relative power of these groups changes with the policies of the particular political party in power and the ideologies these embody. I will discuss the way the relative power of these elements has shifted in the 1980s and 1990s in the next section.

1.4 In Scotland education is administered through the Scottish Office Education Department. The absence of school boards (governors) in many schools and the facts that up to 1992 no school has opted out of local government control and local management of schools has not been implemented leaves regional authorities (equivalent to England and Wales' LEAs) with a more powerful role than south of the border. There are nine regional and three island education authorities in Scotland.

1.5 The Department of Education, Northern Ireland, controls schools through the five education and library boards. Secondary education remains selective, as does segregation according to religious affiliation.

1.6 Besides the elements of the system with legal powers and duties in state education, the education system contains a variety of other groups exerting pressures of varying strength. These include the independent education sector, parents' groups, parent–teacher associations, voluntary organizations, organizations of disabled people, employers, academics, organized religious groups, political pressure groups, and government-established bodies such as the National Curriculum Council and assessment councils.

DES	LEA	Headteacher	Parents	Governors
Policy making	Provide 'adequate and efficient' education at primary and secondary level (nursery optional)	Care of pupils ('*in loco parentis*')	Send child to school (or 'educate otherwise')	Oversee implementation of national curriculum, conduct and discipline‡
Inspecting all schools and institutions (except universities) to ensure standards		Internal organisation of school	Express preference for a school‡	Financial management of school‡
Supply and training of teachers	Establish, alter and close schools (after giving public notice)	Rules, discipline, curriculum (subject to national curriculum and governors' general direction)	Be represented on governing body	Appointment and dismissal of teachers‡
Final court of appeal in disputes between parents and LEA	Finance schools* and local education service		Receive published information about school‡	Suspension/expulsion of pupils
Management of public sector higher education† (via NAB)	Enforce school attendance		Be involved in assessment procedure for children with special educational needs‡	Sex education‡
Providing education support grants†	Student grants (England and Wales)			Use 'best endeavours' to identify children with special educational needs‡
Assisted places scheme†	Identify and provide for special educational needs		Withdraw child from religious instruction	
Financing universities (via UFC) and polytechnics and larger colleges (via PCFC)†	Health and safety		Decide whether a school should 'opt out' of LEA control‡	Publish information for parents about the school‡
Collecting statistics	Careers service			
Educational building programme	Ensure equal opportunities for both sexes and all races			

Figure 1. Powers and duties. An asterisk (*) indicates a power traditionally held by the LEA which can now be taken over by schools which 'opt out'; a dagger (†) indicates new powers which central government has taken on since 1979; often transferred from the LEA; a double dagger (‡) in the parents or governors columns indicates new duties and rights they have received since 1979 (Statham et al. (1991) The Education Fact File, 2nd edn, pp. 85–7, Figure 6.7, Open University).

1.7   The various statutory and other groups have a number of ways of making their influence felt on education:

- Some groups have power because they have been elected to their positions and therefore have a legitimate authority and a duty to formulate and implement educational policy.

- Some groups have power because they have the financial resources to control livelihoods of others.

- Some groups have power because they are sufficiently large in number that their solid voice makes them forceful.

- Some groups have a professional and an emotional investment in the education system that gives them the authority of argument and experience.

- Sometimes groups have power because they have a long history and are seen to be authoritative for this reason.

1.8   But not all power in the education system resides in groups or organizations. Individuals may be powerful either because they are physically dominant or because they are seen as mentally dominant. Others may be powerful because of their personal achievements and success – their 'star' quality.

1.9   Because groups and individuals frequently disagree about what sort of education system would be the 'best', power is not shared but fought for. Power struggles – between government and opposition, between men and women, between people of different races and of different social classes, between children and adults, students and teachers, lay people and professionals – are inevitable as long as interests are seen to clash rather than to coincide and access to wealth, government, information or solidarity remains inequitably constrained.

1.10   The 1988 Education Reform Act (ERA) gave central government unprecedented control over what is taught in schools and how students' work is assessed. It also gave to individual schools unprecedented control over the management of their budgets and staffs. This combination of centralization and decentralization has left the local education authorities with markedly reduced powers and reflects the determination of the Conservative government to abolish inefficient and unwieldy bureaucracies and fatally to weaken the source of some of the most effective opposition to their policies, the Labour-controlled metropolitan and urban councils. Arguments about the future of local education authorities are presented in Section 3 below, but a more extended discussion of their role is the subject of Unit 15.

1.11   Following this introduction there is a section on the educational thinking of the Conservative, Labour and Liberal Democrat parties as set out in their policy documents. Next, Section 3 looks first at those groups who may be losing ground in terms of their power – the bureaucrats and the professionals – and then at those groups who may be gaining ground – the consumers, voluntary organizations and other lay people with an interest in education. Section 4 focuses on the ways in which the power of disabled people has increased as a force within the education system and how they make explicit the links between an education system, society as a whole and the fundamental view of the value of individuals that underlies both.

STUDYING THIS UNIT

1.12   One chapter from Reader 1 and five chapters from Reader 2 support the work in this unit. You will also be asked to watch television programme 7, *Images of Disability*, as part of your study of Section 4. The additional material for each section is as follows:

Section 3 Losing ground and gaining ground?

Reader 2, Chapter 26: 'A curriculum for all: a hard task for some' by Margaret Peter.

Reader 2, Chapter 27: 'A union view of special education policy' by Shirley Darlington.

Reader 2, Chapter 28: 'Empowering the voluntary sector: the campaign for policy change' by Mairian Corker.

Section 4 The politics of disability

Reader 2, Chapter 21: 'The concept of oppression and the development of a social theory of disability' by Paul Abberley.

Reader 2, Chapter 13: 'A hard journey in the right direction: experiencing life beyond an institution' by Linda Shaw.

Reader 1, Chapter 25: 'Blood relations: educational implications of sickle-cell anaemia and thalassaemia' by Simon Dyson.

TV 7: *Images of Disability*.

2 CHANGING POWER-RELATIONSHIPS IN EDUCATION: A BACKGROUND FOR THE 1990S

2.1 In Unit 1/2 Tony Booth argued that the education system is constantly changing and that sources of power and therefore power-relationships fluctuate in response. He noted two particularly striking changes that have occurred during his own working life: first, the rise and fall of local education authorities and, second, the tightening-up of central control over the curriculum, which has, at the same time, broadened out from the old narrow 'funnel' into a 'cylinder'. Headteachers and school governors are in a position to control access to the National Curriculum introduced by the 1988 Education Reform Act because they can exempt students from part or all of the curriculum. It remains to be seen how far they will exercise this power. (See also Section 4 below.)

2.2 Soon after their election victory of 1979, the Conservatives gave priority to 'halting the move to comprehensive education and, at the same time, to shoring up and indeed strengthening the private sector' (Simon, 1991, p. 478). The Education Act of 1980 placed a duty on local education authorities to comply with a parent's choice of school, unless this would mean an inefficient use of resources, and appeals committees were set up to hear parents' complaints. Parents could choose a school outside their own catchment area, thus introducing the principle of open enrolment. The 1980 Act also laid down that a minimum of two parents were to be elected to the governing bodies of schools (see Deem, 1990, pp. 155–6).

2.3 Parental choice cut across the power of local education authorities to put into effect an overall plan in their areas, particularly in the light of falling rolls. A divide between popular and unpopular schools was a likely consequence of this Act, entailing a more inequitable school experience for children and young people. Individual parental choice and increased central control devalued the idea that a school should serve a community of local children, young people and adults.

2.4 The 1986 Education Act further increased the representation of lay people on school governing bodies, whose duties were significantly extended into the areas of implementing the curriculum and appointing staff.

2.5 Centralization of control was increased at this time by means of direct grants for inservice education or for technical and vocational initiatives. The status of professional and 'expert' opinion was reduced by the abolition of the English and Welsh Central Advisory Councils, which had been set up under the 1944 Education Act.

2.6 During the 1980s a series of Education Acts transformed the educational experiences of most children and young people in the United Kingdom. For example, the 1981 Education Act abolished categories of 'handicap', such as 'educationally subnormal', 'maladjusted' and 'delicate', replaced them with the idea of a continuum of 'special educational needs' and introduced a formal assessment procedure, supposed to involve parents as 'equal partners', that could result in the writing of an individual 'Statement' (or 'Record' in Scotland) designed to secure an appropriate and adequately supported curriculum. The Act also allowed – but did not require (nor support with the guarantee of extra resources) – the greater participation within the mainstream of all children and young people, whatever their abilities and interests.

2.7 The 1988 Education Reform Act, in contrast to the 'enabling' character of the 1981 Act, was a prescriptive, 'top-down' piece of legislation, introducing the compulsory National Curriculum and standard attainment targets, local management of schools (LMS), open enrolment and opting out to grant maintained status. This represented a wholesale reshaping of the state system, involving vastly increased powers both for the Secretary of State and the Department of Education and Science and for those running individual schools. The power of local education authorities was attenuated by this polarization and, in as much as it had been the LEAs who organized the networks of support for students seen to have 'special educational needs', this shift in the balance of power would not seem to have been in the students' interests. Indeed, when the Education Reform Bill was first published in 1987, there were no references to students seen as having special educational needs. Amendments had rapidly to be drafted in response to national criticism. These students do not have a high priority with central policy makers.

2.8 Conservative Schools' Minister Michael Fallon outlined his view of the future: 'Our aim, as far as possible, is for independent state schools that need and use local services, pay for them, but in all respects are free to manage their own affairs' (see Sharron, 1991, p. 16).

A CONSERVATIVE CULTURAL REVOLUTION?

The Citizen's Charter

2.9   In July 1991, the Conservative government published the *Citizen's Charter* (Cabinet Office, 1991), heralding a whole series of proposals for consolidating their reforms of the public sector, which included the health service, housing, transport, social services, employment services, the Post Office, the police and the criminal justice system, the Inland Revenue and Customs and Excise departments and, of course, education.

2.10   The charter's subtitle and theme was *raising the standard*, to be achieved by giving responsible citizens more opportunities to make better-informed choices and so have a greater say in how the services they pay for are run. The emphasis was on raising the quality of services through increased competition between private providers.

2.11   However, the government acknowledged that 'essential services – such as education and health – must be available to all, irrespective of means' (Charter, p. 4). They claimed that a complete transformation of public into private services was not envisaged but, as a check on inefficiency and bureaucracy, there were proposals for new central regulatory procedures and individual complaints procedures. The rhetoric was and still is about 'giving more power to citizen' (p. 2) and about the publication of 'full, accurate information' (p. 5) on performance targets and standards achieved.

The Parent's Charter

2.12   The Citizen's Charter contained a two-page outline of a charter for parents (pp. 13–14), which was published in full as a separate booklet by the Department of Education and Science (DES, 1991). It said: 'This is your charter. It will give new rights to you as an individual parent, and give you personally new responsibilities and choices' (back cover). The focus was on the individual parent, as it was on the individual 'citizen'. The main sections included: 'The right to know', 'The right to choose' and 'What to do if things go wrong'.

2.13   A parent's right to know was to be honoured by 'five key documents':

- a report on the individual child or young person
- regular reports on his or her school from independent inspectors (see Section 3, on LEAs and the HMI)
- performance tables published for all local schools
- individual school prospectus or brochure
- school governors' annual report.

2.14   A parent had the 'right to an education which meets any special educational needs your child has' (DES, 1991, p. 12). Parents were reminded of their right to initiate and to be fully involved in the assessment of their children's educational needs. The 'right to choose' for those parents whose children have a statement of special educational needs, however, was restricted compared to that of other parents. The charter said:

> Some pupils are best educated in special schools for all or part of their time at school. They will be pupils who have a statement of special educational needs which says that a special school is more suitable for them than an ordinary primary or secondary school.
> (DES, 1991, p. 12)

2.15   A parent's right to appeal against the recommendations of his or her child's statement was not mentioned here but later, in the section on complaints procedures (DES, 1991, p. 16). As well as the appeals committee members chosen by the local authority or by school governors, the government planned to change the law so that each committee also had one 'independent' member to give parents 'a fair and independent hearing'.

2.16   The Parent's Charter included numerous references to proposals that require a change in the law; in the version published in England these passages were printed in red ink. This was not true for the version published for Scottish parents, and five of the twelve Scottish regions refused to distribute the charter to their schools on the grounds that the document was party political propaganda. DES figures quoted in the *Times Educational Supplement* revealed that the government set aside £4.5 million for advertising and promotion for the year 1991/92. Jack Straw, the Labour Party's spokesman on education, agreed that the charter was propaganda on the grounds that it was based on legislation that had yet to go before the Houses of Parliament (see Hackett, 1992a, p. 3).

League tables

2.17   According to the provisions of the Education (Schools) Bill, which received the Royal Assent in March 1992, information about the quality, standards and efficiency of schools and the destinations of school-leavers was to be published in order to:

(a) assist parents in choosing schools for their children; and

(b) increase public awareness of the quality of the education provided by the schools concerned and of the educational standards achieved in those schools.

(Education (Schools) Bill, cl. 16 (3))

2.18   The introduction of the Education Bill, which was mainly concerned with the future of Her Majesty's Inspectorate (see Section 3), caused a storm of criticism from both sides of the House of Commons and from schools and the civil servants affected by its provisions.

2.19   First, the league tables were criticized for failing to take into account the differences between schools in terms of the abilities and backgrounds of their pupils. For example, a school in which many of the students are bilingual, with English as their second language, may not appear to be performing as well as a neighbouring school, although in fact the progress being made by the students may be greater.

2.20   Secondly, a school in which there is a commitment to increasing the participation of students seen to have 'special educational needs' and in which there is therefore a corresponding commitment to developing curricula that reflect all the students' interests and attainments, may not do as well as a nearby school when it comes to comparing test scores and public examination grades, but it may be doing much better than that other school when it comes to maximizing the potential of all its students. 'Quality' in the government's proposals seems to refer not to quality at all but to the quantity of attainments of universal 'standards'.

2.21   Other critics have argued that, while the aim of publishing information about schools' performance is to raise standards as a consequence of the pressure exerted by parent-citizens, in practice the league tables will prevent this. Because schools are funded according to the number of students on roll, the higher the number of students the more money available to the school. Local education authorities can no longer provide additional funds to support particular schools. So if a school is less popular and therefore has less to spend, it can become trapped in a downward spiral of undesirability, with fewer resources available for raising standards (see Beckett, 1992).

LABOUR'S PROPOSALS: *GOOD EDUCATION FOR ALL*

2.22   In *Meet the challenge. Make the change. Good education for all* (1991), the Labour Party also emphasized the need for quality and high standards and favoured the idea of rewards for exceptionally good practice. Unlike the Conservatives, however, the Labour Party stressed:

- the need to work towards equality and diversity in the education system

- the need to strengthen, rather than weaken, the partnership between parents, teachers, governors, local education authorities and the Secretary of State

- the need for success to be measured in terms of progress rather than exam results

- the need to put an end to selective schooling, which gives children and young people an enhanced or a reduced value depending upon their level of educational attainment: 'Equality requires that every child and adult be treated as of equal worth' (Labour Party, 1991, p. 46).

2.23 The Labour Party argued that:

> Fully comprehensive schools can raise overall standards as well as substantially improve the attainment of working class pupils. ...
>
> Fully comprehensive education also means meeting the varying special needs of the one in five children and young people with physical and mental disabilities or other learning difficulties. We believe that provided the education is appropriate to the needs of the child, the more normal the environment in which the child is educated, the greater the chances of real integration in adult life.
>
> (Labour Party, 1991, p. 48)

2.24 There were limits to their policy of deselection:

> For some children, the particular expertise and facilities of special schools and units will remain the best educational provision. ...
>
> All schools, like independent special schools and others which meet genuine boarding needs and complement, not compete with, LEA provision, will continue to receive public funding.
>
> (Labour Party, 1991, p. 48)

PUTTING PUPILS FIRST: THE ENGLISH LIBERAL DEMOCRATS

2.25 The Liberal Democrats' focus was on the freedom of the individual and the liberating power of education:

> Liberal Democrats believe there is room for an alternative vision of education, based neither on an all-powerful state nor on confused notions of the free market. It is community based, democratically accountable, participative and responsive to changes in consumer demand, social and economic trends and professional advance. Above all, it centres on the needs and wishes of the individual pupil.
>
> (Liberal Democrats, 1990, p. 3)

2.26 Like the Labour Party, the Liberal Democrats supported a comprehensive non-selective system of education, the principle of equality of opportunity and partnerships between schools, their communities and local education authorities. They supported the decentralization of management to the governing bodies of individual schools but rejected the increased powers of the Secretary of State contained in the Education Reform Act (1988):

> The National Curriculum ... is over-prescriptive, over-bureaucratic and under-funded ... The assessment programme is encouraging crude comparisons between schools and not helping to determine the needs and strengths of individual pupils. Above all, the present system is restricting curriculum innovation and development.
>
> (Liberal Democrats, 1990, p. 5)

2.27 Individual resourcing was the theme of the Liberal Democrats' policy towards children and young people seen as having 'special educational needs':

> Individuals with disabilities or special learning needs are particularly dependent upon properly resourced, appropriate education to enable them to lead as normal a life as possible with the community.
>
> (Liberal Democrats, 1990, p. 12)

It was therefore proposed that each local education authority should set up a 'special educational needs service', with its own budget, so that these pupils 'do not have to compete, under LMS, with the provision of better school facilities for other children' (Liberal Democrats, 1990, p. 12). As well as the formal statements of special educational needs that are written for some pupils, the Liberal Democrats proposed an informal 'indicative statement' for pupils whose special needs are less severe, as a way of routing resources to particular individuals.

2.28 Integration was seen as 'desirable', but, echoing the view of the Labour Party:

> only achievable where proper support for the pupil's needs is available. ... There is ... a continuing need for special schools and for specialist units where children spend some time within the unit and some within the mainstream school.
>
> (Liberal Democrats, 1990, p. 12)

CONTRASTING PERSPECTIVES

Activity 1 Perspectives on education

On 9 April 1992 the Conservatives were returned to power with an overall majority of 21. You are reading this unit at some time between 1992 and 2000 and will be familiar with what is happening in the education system as you study. This activity gives you the opportunity to refresh your memory of pre-election promises and chart their course from promise to reality.

Key action-plans for education from the Conservatives, the Labour Party and the Liberal Democrats are reproduced on pages 14–16. Read them and make some notes in answer to the following questions:

- What are the similarities and differences between the education policies of the three parties as reflected in these action-plans?

- What has happened in practice since 1992 and how far has the government been able to put into practice its pre-election commitments?

- What sources are available to you to monitor the implementation of education policy locally and nationally?

A CHARTER FOR PARENTS

The Government's school reforms have had three key purposes:

- to raise standards in education for all pupils;
- to promote parental influence and choice and widen accountability;
- to achieve better use of resources for pupils.

The Citizen's Charter reinforces these principles and carries them further. It will mean:

- **school reports** on the progress of all pupils, at least annually;
- clear publication of **results achieved** in schools;
- easier **comparison of results** between schools;
- **regular and independent inspection** of all schools with the results reported to parents;
- **more information** to parents to help them to exercise the choice that the education reforms have given them.

We believe that all parents are entitled to expect full information about their children's education in terms of the curriculum, achievements, and management of schools.

Reforms already in place give parents:

- *a **national curriculum** for their children that sets clear objectives backed by national tests showing what each individual child is achieving;*
- *fuller representation on the **governing bodies** of schools;*
- *the right to propose to run their own school, through **grant maintained** status, and a greater say, through **local management**, in how **all** schools are run. More of the management of resources and schools must be transferred from LEAs to within the schools themselves;*
- *more choice, through **open enrolment**, about what schools their children attend, and clearer routes to changing schools;*
- ***more information** to help parents choose a school; more information on how their children are performing, and about how it is possible to change schools.*

These reforms are having a beneficial effect on standards in schools and on parental choice. The Citizen's Charter will guarantee further progress.

The Conservatives' Charter for Parents

Labour's plans

- We will ensure that our schools and colleges are adequately resourced. No student should have to rely on parental contributions for basic textbooks and essential equipment.

- All children have the right to be taught in stimulating schools - housed in safe, well-equipped buildings - to give pride to both pupils and parents.

- All children have the right to attend good comprehensive schools offering a broad curriculum. A Labour government will end the assisted places scheme and will incorporate all city technology colleges (CTCs) and opt out schools into the local education authority.

- Labour will provide better training for teachers, so that they receive regular updates on their skills. We also need to tackle the shortage of teachers qualified in maths, physics, craft, design and technology.

- We will provide better quality and choice of education and care for under-fives by integrating provisions such as nursery schools, play groups, day nurseries or child minders.

- Labour will ensure that every parent is part of a 'home school partnership agreement' which outlines the rights and responsibilities of parents and school in the child's education.

- Labour will set targets to improve the number of 16-19 year olds that gain qualifications.

- An education standards council will be established to assist schools and local education authorities to develop proper yardsticks.

- Schools will be regularly inspected and HMIs and local inspectors will be required to set targets for improvement in schools and monitor progress.

- We will give more training and support to parent governors.

- Labour will end the divide in planning and funding between the polytechnic and university sector by creating a single higher and continuing education council.

Labour's plans

- The replacement of the current National Curriculum with a broader and more flexible curriculum framework, and of the rigid assessment of all pupils with Individual Diagnostic Records and Records of Pupil Achievement.

- The extension of Local Management of Schools through the introduction of an annual negotiation between each LEA and its schools over levels and distribution of funding.

- The reincorporation into LEAs of all grant-maintained schools and City Technology Colleges.

- An increased level of funding for the early years of education (3-7 years olds).

- The integration of policy for all LEA post-16 provision - including school sixth forms, further education, tertiary and sixth form colleges - into a coherent whole.

- Compulsory part-time (at least two days a week) education and/or training for all employees aged under 18.

- Investment in adult education and training, particularly in crash courses in the main areas of skill deficiency.

- The establishment of a General Teaching Council, with powers to control professional qualifications and eligibility to teach.

- Nationally negotiated agreements on teachers' pay, which would allow for local initiatives aimed at areas of teacher shortage.

The English Liberal Democrats: Putting Pupils First

2.29   The Conservative government of the 1980s and early 1990s had the advantage of power, of course, and their plans for the future of education included a reminder of the benefits of reforms already set in motion. The context for these plans was the restructuring of the entire public sector. Education was just one the services being re-created in an image which reflected the themes of 'quality, choice, standards, value'.

2.30   The Conservatives appealed to individual citizens and individual parents. They were concerned to reduce the influence of local politicians and professionals. The Labour Party appealed to teachers as well as parents and children and wanted to strengthen the role of local education authorities. The Liberal Democrats were concerned to strengthen local 'community' control of a much more coherent education system; one of the themes in their key recommendations was the provision of adequate funding.

2.31 Labour's plans included the statement that: 'All children have the right to attend good comprehensive schools offering a broad curriculum'. The Liberal Democrats recommended replacing the National Curriculum with a more flexible approach and they wanted to replace standard attainment targets with individualized records of achievement. These two statements reflect a commitment to an inclusive equitable education system, which, as we have seen, includes at least some students identified as having 'special educational needs'.

2.32 The Conservatives' commitment to, on the one hand, a more uniform system of curriculum and assessment and, on the other hand, increased parental choice and control precluded them from making any similar commitment to valuing diversity within rather than between schools. Insofar as they were aiming for a completely independent system and supported the continuation of selective private schools, it could be argued that they were not really interested in *state* education.

3 LOSING GROUND AND GAINING GROUND?

3.1 In this section I look at the changing position of bureaucrats, professionals and consumers and ask what are the implications of shifting power-relationships for parents and children.

LOCAL EDUCATION AUTHORITIES

3.2 The power of LEAs is, in 1992, threatened by:

- the provisions of the 1988 Education Reform Act, particularly the local management of schools (LMS) and opting-out
- the proposals in the Local Government Bill to devolve powers relating to school buildings, for example, to town and parish councils
- the aim of reducing community charge rates, which leaves local authorities with less to spend on education.

3.3 If the Conservative government is charged with being responsible for the decline in the material and educational standards of schools and colleges, the answer comes back that it is the fault of profligate town halls and 'progressive', child-centred classrooms:

> It would be hard to plan the present education provision worse than the councils have done since the war. ...

> I don't think we lose much sleep fretting over the future of the LEAs.
>
> (Schools' Minister, Michael Fallon, quoted in Sharron, 1991, p. 16)

3.4   Now that the Conservatives have been returned to power, they will encourage more schools to opt out, perhaps implementing their 'final solution' to the problem of the LEAs:

> Once the bulk of secondary schools have opted out of local authority control, the Conservatives could rid themselves of troublesome local councils and set up agencies to run networks of primary schools.
>
> (Hackett, 1992b)

3.5   How far organizations resembling local education authorities would need to be reinvented if they are abolished in the next few years remains to be seen. There may be limits to devolution if lay councillors and governors find themselves in need of support in carrying out their unaccustomed tasks of financial management, administration and strategic planning (*TES*, 1992).

HER MAJESTY'S INSPECTORATE

3.6   HMIs have been inspecting schools since 1839, the year in which the Committee of Council for Education, the beginnings of a government education department, was set up and six years after the first state grants were given to the Anglican and Nonconformist denominational societies which ran the elementary schools. One witness who gave the evidence to the Parliamentary Committee on the State of Education in 1834 argued enthusiastically that the thorough inspection of all schools was 'an unspeakable blessing to society' (Maclure, 1979, p. 33).

3.7   One hundred and fifty years later the inspectors still saw themselves as making a uniquely valuable contribution to the maintenance of educational standards (see HMI, 1990).

3.8   However, the government proposed to introduce a register of lay people to act as inspectors and to cut the number of permanent staff HMIs from over 500 to less than 200. School inspections would be carried out by teams provided from private agencies, only the leaders of which would be required to be registered. The reduced core-inspectorate would cease to be a department within the DES and would become a separate department of government. About a quarter of the remaining full-time HMIs would be responsible for the training of their lay colleagues.

3.9   In informal interviews conducted while this unit was in preparation, criticisms of the proposals included the following:

- Agency teams would not have the breadth of first-hand experience of practice across the country nor the resulting extensive networks of contacts that were among the greatest strengths of existing full-time permanent HMI teams.

- Agency teams would not be able to provide the continuity of support provided by the full-time permanent HMI teams.
- The proposals would destroy the coherence of the HMI and prevent the Chief Inspector from being in a position to report on the situation in the country as a whole.
- Schools would choose to buy in a team of inspectors that would be likely to endorse rather than reject their current practice because favourable reports would attract prospective parents; this would subvert rather than reinforce independent inspection.

3.10 On 23 January 1992, HMI members of the civil service union, First Division Association, took the unprecedented step of lobbying the House of Commons to express their opposition to the content of the proposals and the threat to their jobs.

3.11 After rushing the Education (Schools) Bill through the House of Commons to get it onto the statute book before the general election in April 1992, the government suffered a significant setback in the House of Lords. Two amendments were passed on the night of 2 March 1992: first, the proposed right of school governors to choose their own inspectors was removed and, second, the proposal to remove from local education authorities the right of entry to inspect the schools they maintain was rejected. Private inspection teams would still be possible and the threat to HMI jobs remained, but the Lords had seriously damaged the government's plans (see Wintour and Bates, 1992).

THE PERSPECTIVE OF A TEACHING UNION

Activity 2 Policy-making and the National Union of Teachers (NUT)

The collective voice of trade unions was systematically silenced during the 1980s on the grounds that the unions were largely responsible for the country's economic inefficiency. Collective action, such as the withdrawal of labour, is now in the early 1990s rare and unlikely to be effective. What kind of critical response to government policy is therefore left to the unions?

Shirley Darlington is one of the NUT's full-time equal opportunities officers and she has a particular interest in the education of children and young people who experience difficulties in learning or who have a disability. She describes how the NUT has influenced national policy in 'A union view of special education policy', which is Chapter 27 of Reader 2. As you read, consider the following questions:

- What is Shirley Darlington's role, inside and outside the NUT?
- What was the role of the NUT in the 1980s? Has this changed since then?

- What was the NUT's policy in the 1980s on the integration of students seen to have 'special educational needs'? What tensions did this create with regard to related policies within the union? How were these tensions resolved?

- How has the NUT been able to influence the development of a national special education policy?

3.12 Shirley Darlington has to keep herself well informed on all the issues relevant to her particular policy areas, so that she can confidently brief the union's executive members. She also has to facilitate the exchange of information for a number of different groups: union members, other voluntary organizations and a variety of people involved in special education. She undertakes individual casework, political lobbying and the monitoring of the implementation of legislation. She has acted as the coordinator of the alliance within the union between those who saw special education as a professional issue, requiring the attention of specialists, and those who saw it as a social and political issue of relevance to everyone.

3.13 The union's advisory committee for special education has been cautious in its support for integration because of fears about inadequate resourcing in the mainstream and because of a commitment to special schools as centres of relevant expertise. This was at odds with the union's commitment to equal opportunities, particularly to equality of access to the mainstream for teachers with disabilities. The increasing solidarity of disabled teachers within the union has enabled and developed a more coherent union view.

3.14 Near the end of the chapter, Shirley Darlington tells us that she was particularly pleased that the NUT secured an amendment to the Education Reform Bill, saying that local education authorities must explicitly make provision for meeting special educational needs in their budget formula. She had personally worked very hard to push this through and she feels strongly that pupils should be supported in the mainstream. However, there are passages in the chapter where I felt that Shirley Darlington's own voice and views did not come across so clearly. Her account of the union's debate about special education, for example, struck me as ambivalent:

> The delicate balancing act between support for the principle of integration – which was felt to be a right for children and which would enable them to integrate more easily into adult life – and the fears about under-resourcing continued, and were borne out in the experiences of schools during the 1980s. Children were being placed in mainstream schools without adequate planning and preparation, and cuts in resources generally made for a hostile climate to successful integration. Members who had been looking to the union for advice and support became angry at what they saw as a confidence trick played by the government on children with special

needs, their parents and teachers. We received many complaints about under-resourced integration which over-burdened teachers who were not adequately trained to deal effectively with pupils with disabilities and learning difficulties, previously found in special schools. ...

The 'casework' approach was successful in some cases, but not with unsympathetic LEAs who were using integration as a means of saving money without adequate safeguards for teachers or pupils. Anger was expressed in such LEAs (for example, Bradford) which moved towards integration on the cheap – not just on behalf of overstretched teachers, but on behalf of children with special needs who were being sold out.

3.15 In this extract, Shirley Darlington seems to be agreeing with the view that integration is not worth pursuing if resourcing is inadequate, rather than with the view she takes later that integration is a right for all students and that all students can adequately be resourced within a single diverse mainstream.

3.16 Perhaps her own commitment grew as the debate developed or perhaps her position within the union made it hard for her to write personally rather than as a spokesperson for a group which contained a divergence of opinion.

THE NATIONAL CURRICULUM COUNCIL

3.17 The National Curriculum Council was set up in 1988 to prepare detailed non-statutory guidance on curriculum development following the passage of the Education Reform Act. Although formally independent, the NCC is funded and has its members appointed by the DES. The working parties convened to tackle individual subjects and cross-curricular themes have consisted of teachers, academics, business people, other relevant professionals, celebrities and journalists. At the time of writing, the new chair of the NCC is David Pascall, a BP executive and former Downing Street adviser. One journalist described his appointment as a move by Kenneth Clarke 'to extricate the National Curriculum Council from the grip of an educational establishment suspected of subverting government proposals' (Bates, 1992, p. 3). The powers of an independent NCC would seem to be circumscribed in practice.

Activity 3 A working party

Margaret Peter, editor of the *British Journal of Special Education*, was co-opted onto the NCC's Special Educational Needs Task Group (SENTG) early in 1989. Like the Education Reform Bill, the first three reports to come out of the NCC, on science, mathematics and English, did not address the issue of students who experience difficulties in learning or who have a disability; Kenneth Baker, then Secretary of State, had rejected the proposal for the inclusion within every working group of someone with relevant knowledge and expertise. The SENTG was hurriedly set up in response to the loud calls for advice from practitioners across the country and *A Curriculum for All – Special Needs in the National Curriculum* was published in September (NCC, 1989b). The emphasis is on 'access', 'entitlement' and a minimal use of the provisions of the Education Reform Act to exempt pupils from or disapply the National Curriculum.

Now read 'A curriculum for all: a hard task for some' by Margaret Peter, which is Chapter 26 of Reader 2. As you read consider the following questions:

- What was the task of the group?
- Who was seen as the audience of the final report?
- Why was the experience so stressful for Margaret Peter and her colleagues?
- How free was Margaret Peter to express her own views?
- If you have ever been involved in a similar joint exercise, what did you notice about the operation of power-relationships, both inside and outside the working group?

3.18   The task of the group was huge: first to define what was meant by 'access' and then to present ways of making science, maths and English accessible to students of all abilities and all ages for a wide audience of professional workers in both mainstream and special schools. Moreover, as the group was obliged to present its report in advance of the implementation of the National Curriculum, there was very little in the way of relevant good and innovatory practice for them to learn from or use as examples. Margaret Peter describes the pressure to 'act now, think later'.

3.19   Apart from the lack of time and the complexity of the task, there were the stresses of writing in collaboration with a large team, the endless drafting, and the pressure to respond to the interests both of the commissioning politicians and of the professional audience. Further, any large group will contain differences of view that would have to be reconciled if a unanimous report was to be possible.

3.20   Margaret Peter tells us that she had been critical of the Education Reform Bill when it was going through parliament, but that now it was law

> It must be made to work. ... Whatever could be done to reassure teachers that pupils with special needs would not be stranded on the sidelines of change was worth doing.

(Reader 2, p. 306)

This was the new challenge and did not have to entail the suspension of her critical approach.

3.21 The power remained, of course, with the government and the DES throughout, not with the professional 'experts' in the advisory group.

CONSUMERS

Parent-power?

3.22 The Conservatives aimed to reduce the power of tenured bureaucrats and public service professionals, while enhancing that of 'citizens' and 'consumers'. In education, consumer power is to be increased through parental choice, open enrolment and local management by school governing bodies. At least, that is the rhetoric. In reality, the different strands of policy may conflict. For example, in an area in which a large proportion of the secondary schools have opted out of LEA control, the power over who goes to which school may in practice belong to the school, which will be free to operate selection procedures that do not suit the full range of prospective parents.

3.23 If individual grant maintained schools do decide to become selective by perceived ability, then not only does this go against the last echo of the idea of community preserved in the Parent's Charter, in which enrolment is seen in terms of proximity to the school and whether or not a child's siblings go there, but it seriously reduces the options of those parents who either do not want their children to go to a school which selects according to attainment or whose children might not gain a place. It seriously reduces the options of parents who want a local mainstream place for children who have statements of special educational needs. A school's policy on selection may, in this way, work counter to the right of parents to choose a school for their children.

Headteachers and school governors

3.24 The 1986 Education Act increased parent and community representation on school governing bodies and decreased that of the local education authority (see above). The 1988 Education Reform Act introduced local management and a range of weighty new duties for governors, including:

- financial management
- the hiring, firing and rewarding of staff
- operating the school's admissions policy
- deciding whether or not to apply for grant maintained status
- ensuring the school conforms to the regulations for the implementation of the National Curriculum and the assessment strategy.

3.25 Two issues have so far emerged as particularly problematic: the relative power of governors and headteachers, and the burdensome responsibility for complex financial decisions in the context of having to implement cuts.

3.26 When lay and professional members of a governing body find themselves in dispute, what issues should be taken into consideration in the search for a resolution? For example, what should be the extent of the power of the chair of the governing body of a school? Should the chair ever act as an individual or as the representative of a minority group rather than as the delegate of the governing body as a whole? Should the chair exercise control over the professional concerns of headteachers and their staff? Should headteachers expect to consult the governors about the detail of their work and about such things as the professional appraisal of their staff?

3.27 It could be argued that one of the not-so-hidden agendas for governing schools was that lay governors should become involved in the internal running of their schools. It could also be argued that the opportunity for parents and other lay people to develop an educational relationship with their local schools is long overdue. It depends how far you believe that an educational relationship is possible under the terms of the Education Reform Act. Writing in *Forum* magazine, Nanette Whitbread expressed her view that the Act

> subverted the nascent development of a shared partnership model for the co-operative management of schools ... It introduced an ideology of competitive market forces into an enterprise that is properly concerned with co-operative planning for the educational benefit of children.
>
> (Whitbread, 1992)

3.28 Another issue is whose community a school should be seen as representing. Should any school see its community as consisting of a single constituency of students, even in areas where this could be seen as a way of combating negative discrimination, for example against minority ethnic groups?

3.29 In Liverpool, a dispute between the governors and the staff at a secondary school resulted in the sacking of the chair of the governors for his 'interference ... in the proper business of the headteacher' (Frank Cogley, Liverpool's Director of Education, quoted in *TES*, 1 November 1991, p. 2). The bureaucrats intervened to support the professionals.

Voluntary organizations: developing a role in policy-making

3.30 There are other ways in which people may act collectively to try to influence education policy-making in their own interests. Here is an example of the consumers of services organizing themselves to develop a critical voice loud enough and credible enough to influence decision-making and resource allocation.

Activity 4 Policy-making and the National Deaf Children's Society

Now read 'Empowering the voluntary sector: the campaign for policy change' by Mairian Corker, which is Chapter 28 in Reader 2.

Mairian Corker works for the National Deaf Children's Society (NDCS) and is deaf herself. As you read the article, consider the following questions:

- What are the dilemmas for charitable voluntary organizations in the 1990s?
- What is Mairian Corker's role in the NDCS and what dilemmas does she face as an individual worker?
- What view of integration does the NDCS support?
- How has the NDCS been able to influence national policy?
- What are the implications for the voluntary sector of the empowerment of disabled children and adults and their families?

3.31 One of the dilemmas for voluntary organizations like the NDCS is the tension between the gift of services to a client group and the assertion of a right to services by the client group. A gift allows power to remain with the donor and does not disturb the status quo. Accepting that recipients have a right to services, on the other hand, would entail a shift in power away from the donors towards the recipients. So as societies like the NDCS move towards the acceptance of the rights of disabled people, their own existence becomes threatened. Attention shifts to lobbying for a comprehensive state system which does not have to be supplemented by a voluntary sector.

3.32 Another dilemma arises as the voluntary sector becomes more professional in its management and so more powerful as a critic of government policy. Mairian Corker argues that: 'it is itself becoming involved in the same market philosophy which has led to existing policy' (p. 333).

3.33 A third dilemma for Mairian Corker arises from the pressure on the NDCS to hold back from a whole-hearted commitment to the acceptance of British Sign Language (BSL) as a minority language by the DES because of the need to please all its members, which include hearing parents of deaf children, who may not support this policy. The power of the NDCS therefore has to reflect the extent of consensus between its different members.

3.34 The NDCS helps individual children and parents to secure the education that they themselves want and has provided effective advocacy in appeals against statements of special educational needs that families saw as inadequate or inappropriate. Mairian Corker wants to empower children and families, presenting professionals with intellectual challenges as well as politicians with new principles for policy-making.

3.35   Apart from working with individual families, Mairian Corker sees the challenging of 'disabling policies and attitudes' (p. 324) as a core activity. She believes that adherence to a medical model of deafness has resulted in the discrimination experienced by deaf children. She argues for a 'functional' view, which sees deafness as normal and allows professionals to focus on communication skills, awareness training and equal opportunities rather than on audiology and compensatory speech and language work. Society has to adapt to the people within it, not the other way round. Powerless minorities should not have to assimilate to the dominant majority.

3.36   The NDCS has made some impact on the implementation of legislation, but has not been very effective in lobbying for a significant change of policy during the 1980s. Also, Mairian Corker describes how 'partnerships' between voluntary organizations and professionals do not work as between equals. Agendas are controlled by the professionals and controversial issues can therefore be omitted.

CONCLUSION: WHERE DOES THIS LEAVE PARENTS AND CHILDREN?

3.37   In this section I have looked at those with an interest in education whose power has declined as a result of government policy and at those groups whose power the Conservative government said would increase as a result of their reforms: consumers, parents, governors, voluntary societies. It is not at all clear, however, that these increases will materialize. Further, the reforms may turn out to be in conflict, which will reduce the possibilities for parents to exercise their new rights; the reforms may usher in a system of such complexity that the professionals will be asked by their lay partners to re-assert their authority.

3.38   Area-wide provision, such as support services and inservice education, are threatened by the reduction in the powers of the local education authorities. Grant maintained schools pose a threat to parental choice as they develop their own admissions policies. League tables, if they are to consist of crude test scores without any qualitative information about the progress of students, may discourage schools from welcoming students with a broad range of interests and abilities. School governing bodies are still likely to be controlled by the full-time professionals. Any real swing in the balance of power towards parents and children therefore seems illusory.

3.39   In the next section I am going to look in more detail at some of the ways in which disabled people have nonetheless attempted to take control of their lives and develop a political programme for a society in which they would want to live.

4 THE POLITICS OF DISABILITY

4.1 This section is supported by three reader articles and a television programme and therefore consists largely of a series of activities. First of all, I shall ask you to consider how disabled people can overcome their experiences of physical and social oppression. Secondly, I shall look at how a policy of 'care in the community' can help and hinder people in participating in ordinary life outside an institution. Thirdly, I shall look at the educational implications of a group of inherited blood disorders for people whose ethnicity may have already lead to experiences of powerlessness. Then I shall ask you to watch the television programme *Images of Disability* and examine arguments for and against the poster campaigns of two charitable voluntary organizations that aim to work for specific groups of disabled people. These campaigns raise millions of pounds but for some disabled people the personal, social and political price is too high. The section concludes with a look at the arguments for anti-discrimination legislation and discusses possible reasons why the last Private Member's Bill (1991), which had cross-party support, failed to make progress through the House of Commons.

4.2 The disabled people whose lives you will learn about in this section can be included in the categories of 'citizens' and 'consumers of education'. They are lay members of the community, parents, students, potential school governors. Yet they do not feel that they are gaining political ground.

DISABILITY AND OPPRESSION

4.3 In Unit 11/12 Tony Booth discusses the way some groups are devalued in schools. How far do disabled people have to overcome negative assumptions before their identity as ordinary citizens can be recognized and valued? How far will alliances of disabled people and parents enable them to take power within the education system?

Activity 5   Disability and oppression

Now read 'The concept of oppression and the development of a social theory of disability' by Paul Abberley, which is Chapter 21 of Reader 2. It will remind you of many of the issues which were considered in Unit 10. As you read, consider the following questions:

- What is Paul Abberley's view of the common meanings of 'impairment' and of 'power'? What does he see as the roots of these definitions? What are his proposals for the redefinition of impairment and power?

Images of disability?

"Just because I couldn't speak, they thought I had nothing to say."

MY NAME IS JENNY.
I HAVE CEREBRAL PALSY.
BUT THANKS TO THIS WORD
PROCESSOR, I'VE NOW GOT
A SAY IN MY FUTURE.

THE SPASTICS SOCIETY
It's not that people don't care, it's just that they don't think.

AND YOU THOUGHT IT JUST PARALYSED.

MS MULTIPLE SCLEROSIS
WITHOUT YOUR HELP IT'S INCURABLE

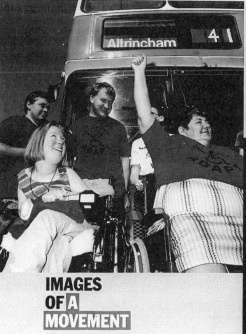

- Is Paul Abberley's analysis adequate to account for the experiences of disabled people?
- What might you want to add to his discussion?

4.4 Paul Abberley views society as composed of hierarchies of power based on class, race and gender. He argues that the complex social and historical contexts for these power-relationships are frequently denied in favour of a simple medical model of disability which devalues individual disabled peoples' lives and ignores the possibilities for their collective empowerment.

4.5 Paul Abberley argues for a recognition of the social factors which underlie the oppression of disabled people and for a transformation of health and welfare provision into a system that can liberate those who need its support. He argues for a theory of disability as oppression, which overturns the medical ideology and which should be seen as an active political project.

CARE IN THE COMMUNITY: CITIZENS OR CLIENTS?

4.6 Ever since the barbaric living conditions for children and adults in long-stay hospitals were revealed in the late 1960s and 1970s by writers like Ann Shearer (1980) and Maureen Oswin (1978), the rhetoric of 'care in the community' has gathered momentum. If all those who have lived in institutions were returned to ordinary communities, this would indeed be a transformation of welfare services. But it is debatable whether such a move would in fact represent an end to the oppression of disabled people and those who have been and are still called 'mentally handicapped'. There are three kinds of arguments in favour of a policy of care in the community but they have different moral bases and social consequences.

4.7 The first argument asserts that long-stay institutions were dehumanizing, that the civil rights of former inmates must be recognized and that statutory community-based services must be developed to maximize their participation in ordinary life.

The second argument asserts that it is desirable, as well as necessary in a time of recession, to make substantial savings in public expenditure and that people should rely on informal networks of family (mostly female) care and voluntary services or use the proliferating private sector and not expect the state to take responsibility.

The third argument asserts that people do not need pre-planned services so much as a guaranteed income and that only the freedom of choice that comes with a personal income can enable people actively to participate in their communities rather than continuing to be dependent clients, users of services over which they have no control.

4.8 The pattern of community care that has evolved over the past twenty-odd years does not clearly reflect the values of any one of the three approaches that I have outlined. There are statutory services, voluntary services, private services, family carers and campaigning users' groups. Carers and cared-for do not have political clout, being economically unproductive, predominantly female and largely excluded from decision-making. Many people have found that the 'community' is hostile, that their new life outside an institution is more lonely, poverty-stricken and insecure than their old life inside. For example:

> Major changes have taken place in the structure and administration of social security benefits which have eclipsed the long-awaited review of social security benefits for disabled people and which have resulted in reduced levels and security of income. These changes have also resulted in a major loss of autonomy and choice in relation to personal care and practical help which disabled people may need to live independently. Entitlements to allowances towards the extra costs of disability, for private help in the home and for residential care have been removed. Resources necessary to pay for the extra costs of disabled living or for personal help are now available only from cash-limited, discretionary, quasi-independent funds and, from April 1993, after scrutiny by social workers and other professionals.
>
> (Glendinning, 1991, p. 16)

Activity 6 Living in the community

Now read 'A hard journey in the right direction: experiencing life beyond an institution' by Linda Shaw, which is Chapter 13 of Reader 2. As you read, consider the following questions:

- How was 'community care' defined by the local health authority in whose area Elizabeth and Helen now live?

- What were the advantages and disadvantages for Elizabeth and Helen of living in the community?

- How did Linda Shaw perceive her role as a support worker and what were the perceptions of Elizabeth and Helen?

- Why was the women's support network so fragile?

- Are Elizabeth and Helen citizens or clients?

4.9 The local health authority's stated principles of community care were: 'community presence, community participation, competence, respect and choice' (p. 161). Elizabeth and Helen spent a good deal of their time in their flat engaged in daily routines, which took longer if they received a minimum of help. To be 'competent', they had to have enough time. This obviously restricted their opportunities to go out and about but they were beginning to attend a variety of adult education classes and to make a few trips and excursions.

4.10   Linda Shaw was paid to be a support worker for Elizabeth and Helen but she was also their friend. One of the problems for her was that the two women did not recognize this distinction. Their attitude raised the issue, for example, of how far she should go in expressing her affection or in behaving like a family member. When one of the women said, 'It's my job!' she was saying something about her position as the occupier of the flat, that it was her home, as it was not for Linda and the other workers. But when one of the women said, 'She can do it!' this seemed less acceptable, treating the worker like a servant, disrespectful, taking away the worker's autonomy by asserting control herself. Control and 'independence' may have more to do with taking decisions than with the performance of certain self-care routines.

4.11   One of the difficulties for Elizabeth of moving from an institution to the community was that the high esteem she had enjoyed 'inside' was not extended automatically on the outside. She felt a loss of security and identity. One of the difficulties experienced by Helen was having to accept personal care from a series of temporary support workers whom she did not know. Nevertheless, both women feel that the move was positive and have no wish to return to hospital.

4.12   The support network seems full of holes. Linda Shaw found that the pay and conditions compromised her own independence and she found the intermingling of the roles of 'worker' and 'friend' disturbing. At the level of the local authority, cuts in public expenditure prevented any improvement in conditions for support workers, and vacant jobs went unfilled. Linda Shaw also describes how the senior professionals who should have been providing support for the support workers in the community were inaccessible.

4.13   Elizabeth and Helen require a range of services but their lives are at the mercy of a very unreliable network. To this extent they are dependent clients. On the other hand, their lives are becoming more autonomous and they are becoming more decisive. How far they could go in the management of their own resources and in the organization of their involvement in the community outside their flat is not known.

DEVALUED IDENTITIES

4.14   Elizabeth and Helen need practical support, but providing adequate support for adults who experience difficulties with everyday tasks has a low status, reflecting that of both client-citizens and support workers.

4.15   Another example is the lack of relevant services for people who have sickle cell anaemia or thalassaemia, inherited blood disorders that are mainly found in black or Mediterranean and Asian communities respectively. Families have received disproportionately inadequate support, compounding their deprivation and strengthening negative stereotypes to which they are expected to conform (see Black and Laws, 1986).

Activity 7 Racism in resourcing for health and education

In 'Blood relations: educational implications of sickle-cell anaemia and thalassaemia', which is Chapter 25 of Reader 1, Simon Dyson tells us that about 75 children with sickle-cell anaemia and about 58 children with thalassaemia are born in the United Kingdom each year. As you read the chapter, consider the following questions:

- Why is the funding for research, treatment and support services so inadequate?

- What are the educational implications for people with sickle-cell anaemia and thalassaemia?

- How can the difficulties that children and young people face at school be overcome?

4.16 Simon Dyson points out that funding for research into sickle-cell anaemia and thalassaemia is far less than for other conditions which affect comparable numbers of people; he suggests that this is because they are disorders rarely found in the white, Northern European population. It is also the case that communities in which sickle-cell anaemia and thalassaemia are found have been reluctant to stress a racially specific disorder for fear of fuelling racist attitudes. Simon Dyson has worked with the Leicestershire organizations of people with sickle-cell anaemia and thalassaemia to press for statutory funding and to raise the awareness of professionals in health, education and social services.

4.17 Richard Fenton describes what it is like to have sickle-cell disease:

> There was nobody to tell me or my mother about what to do, how to cope with it, what to do in winter, how to prevent a crisis. And this went on for years and years, even at school. I remember at school that we had to go out on the playing field in the middle of winter, playing football. And even though I told the teachers that I shouldn't be playing this game because, one, its too exhausting for me and secondly, it's too cold, they wouldn't believe me. And the reason for that was because we didn't have any community support there, or there wasn't any information about sickle-cell anaemia. The thing about sickle-cell anaemia is the unpredictability of it. ... I remember one time when I was about eighteen and I was at home and the pain started. First of all it starts slowly, and then the next thing you know you're on the floor crawling around in pain. You're on your hands and knees and you're in that position for a minute, but that's no good because the pain is too strong. So you stand up. And when you stand up you're twisting around and you're turning

around, and that is no good. And you have to wait for the doctor to come which could be a couple of hours or even longer. And then when he does come he doesn't know what to do...

(quoted in Dyson, 1988, p. 39)

4.18   Katerina Loizi describes what it is like to have thalassaemia:

> My earliest memories of my childhood about having thalassaemia was the pain. The pain when the doctors were trying to find a vein to put a drip up ... Even now I cringe at the thought of having my blood transfusion ... I attended a special school because the authorities felt that I should. ... Personally I don't think I needed to go to special school. I felt different. I was picked up by a coach and I was taken to school. ... And I got teased when I was younger. And I felt alienated about this. Although it was a good school I just felt I should never have gone there.

(quoted in Dyson, 1988, p. 25)

4.19   Pain, exhaustion and frequent absences from school indicate the need for flexible and imaginative support in school for students with sickle-cell anaemia and thalassaemia, but widespread ignorance of them and the cutting-back of LEA-based support services under LMS are major obstacles. A focus on academic studies is in the interests of students with sickle-cell anaemia and thalassaemia, as employment involving physical labour is not appropriate, but if the students are seen as stereotypical under-achievers then teachers' expectations may be far too low and they may stress inappropriate non-academic subjects. Raising awareness of both sickle-cell anaemia and thalassaemia is an issue of combating negative discrimination in school. In Leicestershire, the organizations of people with sickle-cell anaemia and thalassaemia have begun to influence the provision of appropriate health services.

DISABILITY AND CHARITY

4.20   There seems to be no shortage of money, however, to perpetuate the negative image of disabled people: words and pictures that portray them as different kinds of human beings, fearful and tragic specimens from whom it is best to keep a healthy distance, are still common. They are big business. The largest of the national charities make millions of pounds every year from their poster campaigns. Organizations of disabled people are becoming increasingly vociferous in their condemnation of this imagery but a frequent defence by the charities is that this is the best way to capture the attention of an uninformed public. This presents a dilemma for charities, because they rely on their donors for survival but also need to be seen to respond to the demands and comments of their client groups.

Activity 8 Images of disability

Throughout the course, we encourage you to take a critical, independent and personal view of the material that you come across, whether verbal (written or spoken) or visual (moving or still; black and white or in colour). Unit 10 provides a detailed framework for reading texts critically. In television programme 7, *Images of Disability*, I have tried to extend this approach to visual material – words and pictures that you can see every day on hoardings, public transport, television and in the cinema. The programme introduces you to the arguments for and against advertising by national charities. You will see and hear the officers of two charities, the Spastics Society and the Multiple Sclerosis (MS) Society, their advertising agents and disabled adults, who comment on the effect of charitable fund-raising on those whom they are intended to help. You will be presented with different interpretations of the same image, for example two Spastics Society posters and the MS Society's 'Tear Campaign' (see page 28). After a series of illustrated debates, the programme concludes with an alternative approach to raising both public awareness and the power of disabled people to take control over their own lives.

As you watch the programme, consider the following questions:

- What arguments do the charities and their advertising agents put in support of their campaigns? What arguments do disabled adults put in opposition? With whom do you agree?

- Can charities avoid perpetuating a negative image of disability? If not, what sort of support network should succeed them?

- Why are the national charities so powerful in the 1990s?

4.21 The charities give quantitative justifications for their advertising campaigns, which bring millions of pounds. Richard Brewster of the Spastics Society acknowledges that the old patronizing images had to go and he argues that the images that have been developed during the 1980s are dignified by comparison. He thinks the images have to be bold in order to reach the uninformed public and that disabled people are mistaken in thinking that the state is going to take over from the charities and accept what amounts to a Bill of Rights – he believes they oversimplify a very complex issue.

4.22 The MS Society argues that they would be failing their members if they did not raise as much as possible for research and for the provision of welfare services. Alan Ayres, the MS Society's advertising agent, argues that as MS is such an awful disease the forcefulness of the imagery is justified. For him it is like 'Beauty and the Beast'. For the charities, the ends of raising millions of pounds justify the means.

4.23 Jane Campbell rejects these quantitative arguments. For her, the selling of fear and tragedy cannot be justified. The millions of pounds cannot justify the loss of self-esteem and social isolation that is confirmed by the advertising images; the price is too high and the millions must therefore be forgone.

4.24   David Hevey rejects the medical model of disability which, he argues, is strengthened by the charities' approach to advertising. He argues that the handicaps faced by disabled people are rooted in social not individual factors and that images of disabled people can and should be positive: mobile, colourful, sociable. David Hevey criticizes the use of perfect naked bodies in the MS campaigns, which he sees as offensive, sexist and violent, representing disability as the destruction of a normal body, a kind of voyeurism sanctioned because of the medical overtones.

4.25   The actors in the No Excuses theatre company also reject the images put out by the charities and aim to make a political intervention by means of comedy and entertainment. They say that being disabled in our society is quite a 'hilarious' position to be in.

4.26   If it is true that a certain kind of imagery brings in large sums of money that can provide services that would not otherwise exist, then to argue that the negative effects of that imagery are too damaging entails accepting that essential services might cease. Some disabled people are willing to take that risk and keep up the pressure on the government to guarantee an appropriate system. If these services are aimed at those very people who say that they are willing to take the risk, then what could be the justification for not listening to them and putting a stop to the imagery that they condemn?

4.27   I find the arguments put forward by Jane Campbell and David Hevey convincing. To say this, of course, is to make a political statement. The charities are powerful because of their wealth and because the emphasis has been on the provision of private and voluntary services to meet the needs of minority groups, with the state taking minimum responsibility. If you agree with these policies, then you will probably agree that the charitable advertising campaigns are justified, even though you may also accept the criticisms of disabled people. If, on the other hand, you would like to see the functions of the charities taken over by the state and services developed that are shaped by their users, who have access to them as of right, then you will also be willing to risk the millions.

4.28   The Campaigns and Parliamentary Affairs Department of the Spastics Society published the results of a survey of the press (Smith and Jordan, 1991) with a preface by Chris Davies, whose photograph by David Hevey you saw in the television programme. The authors conclude:

> What cannot be denied is the negative way in which people with disabilities are often portrayed. ...
>
> We believe that this negative portrayal is part of the discrimination and exploitation that disabled people experience on a daily basis. Whether it be in the labour market, in the political decision making

process, in service provision and other community resources, people with disabilities are continually refused access, and have their rights denied. The images created by newspapers are found to reflect and reinforce this. The usual defence that the stories published merely reflect the news, and/or are in the public's 'best interest', can no longer be used as an excuse for biased and insensitive journalism.

(Smith and Jordan, 1991, p. 23)

So there may be contradictory activities going on within a single organization: an advertising campaign that the client group finds offensive and a survey whose published findings agree with the clients.

DISABILITY AND POLITICAL REFORM

4.29 At the beginning of this section you read Paul Abberley's article about his theory of disability as oppression. Then you read about two women who are living outside an institution for the first time in their nearly-middle-aged lives. The discussion of each of these articles raises the question of the need for legislative recognition of the discrimination faced by disabled people. There is legislation intended to protect the rights of women and the members of minority ethnic groups, but there is no equivalent for disabled people, whose standard of living and access to employment, housing, health and social services and leisure and recreational activities continue to be disproportionately low.

4.30 Arguments put forward against anti-discrimination legislation include the following:

- 'Disability' is hard to define, the legislation would be difficult to draft and the operation of such an Act would involve people in having to assert their disability rather than their abilities.

- It is better to use persuasion and education to raise awareness of the issue of discrimination and for a pattern of voluntary services to evolve. A 'carrot' is better than a 'stick', and a central commitment comes under the heading of a 'stick'. (In the USA, where anti-discrimination legislation was passed in 1990, this commitment is called 'affirmative action'.)

- Such legislation, unlike that on race and gender, has implications for expenditure, which the government cannot afford and therefore should not be committed to in advance.

4.31 However, since 1982, a number of anti-discrimination measures have been introduced into parliament as Private Member's Bills (see Barnes, 1991, pp. 235–6), but none of them have made it onto the statute book. A Civil Rights (Disabled Persons) Bill (1991) was introduced into the House of Commons by Alf Morris and contained the following definition of disability, taken from United States Public Law 101–336, the Americans with Disabilities Act (1990). 'Disability', with respect to a person, means:

(a) a physical or mental impairment that substantially limits one or more of the major life activities of that person; or

(b) a history of having had such an impairment; or

(c) a reputation as a person who has or had such an impairment.
(Part I, cl. 1(1))

4.32   'Discrimination' is also hard to define but it is said to exist if a disabled person is treated by someone 'less favourably than in identical or similar circumstances he treats or would treat a person who does not have such a disability' (cl. 2). Notions of what is 'reasonable' (usually in financial terms) and 'safe' are included in the Bill and could, presumably, be used as a let-out by employers and service providers.

4.33   The Bill was 'talked out' in the House of Commons in the early hours of 31 January 1992 by the MP for Kingswood, Robert Haywood, who told the Commons that, in 1985, he was diagnosed as having multiple sclerosis. Sometime after two o'clock in the morning, he said:

> Legislation is not required at this stage and I believe that not only because of my own personal experience, but because of my experience as an employer. Reference has been made to the quota system and to the green card. The green card system has not worked over decades. Exemptions have been sought and employers have found ways round it, disregarded it and abused it. It was well-intentioned legislation. I now look for a change in attitude in society as a whole which should be achieved and should continue to be pressed for without legislation.

(Hansard, 31 January 1992, p. 1260)

4.34   Colin Barnes, research officer for the British Council of Organisations of Disabled People (BCODP), disagrees. In his book *Disabled People in Britain and Discrimination* (1991), Colin Barnes argues that there is deep-rooted institutional discrimination against disabled people and that legislation is necessary to enforce a recognition of their rights. For such a measure to be effective, there would need to be:

> comprehensive anti-discrimination legislation which (a) establishes a suitable framework to enforce policies ensuring the integration of disabled people into the mainstream economic and social life of the community, such as employment quota scheme, and (b) provides public confirmation that discrimination against disabled people for whatever reason is no longer tolerable. This would need to be legislation emphasising social rights rather than individual needs, and focusing on a disabling society and not individual disabled people.

(Barnes, 1991, p. 232)

4.35   Colin Barnes believes that Britain cannot afford *not* to implement anti-discrimination legislation. It would not only maximize the contribution that disabled people can make to social and economic life, but also similarly release their present informal, unpaid carers:

The loss to the community in terms of wasted human resources is vast, and it is a loss which will dramatically increase over the next few years. ... The numbers of disabled people will grow. Policies that fail to address discrimination against the disabled are no longer simply morally reprehensible; they are likely to prove economically damaging.

(Barnes, 1992)

Activity 9 Why is anti-discrimination legislation resisted?

The failure of anti-discrimination measures to date raises a number of issues about power-relationships. Here are some points that have occurred to me. Read through my list and then spend a few minutes jotting down your responses.

- Recognizing the rights of people who have been relatively powerless has implications for an altered balance of power, which the encouragement of attitude change by means of education does not.

- If people exercise newly recognized rights, then there would not be the same political space for the exercise of power by those people who have enjoyed it up to now. So opposition to anti-discrimination legislation may not be the result, solely, of hostility to the content of the proposals but also of resistance to their formal implications.

- If people in power are therefore unlikely to give it up or share it, even when they agree, for example, that disabled people do face negative discrimination, then those who experience a denial of their rights will have to take power for themselves and assert their role in political decision-making. There has been much discussion in this course of the 'empowerment' of disabled people, but if you try to do this for someone else it will turn out to be patronage – deliberately or unintentionally.

Compile a list of your own points. How would you set about arguing for anti-discrimination legislation?

5 CONCLUSION: FINDING YOUR WAY AROUND THE SYSTEM

5.1 In this unit I have presented a range of examples of the kinds of power-relationships that affect the education system. You will be able to chart from your own perspective of time and place how these relationships may be evolving and evaluate changes against the yardstick of your own commitments. Who controls the educational decision-making, information networks and resource allocation locally and nationally?

5.2   The language that is used to talk about the education system has been transformed over the past decade or so, but is there any real transformation in the nature of the power-relationships that exist? Do the consumers of educational services really have the main say in how the system is run? It seems to be the case that the power of civil servants has been reduced, but will this only be temporary? And, if their power has not in practice passed on to the 'citizens', where has it been concentrated? Can you detect any permanent changes in the balance of power in education? Perhaps the alliances of disabled people, their families and their supporters represent a constituency that will refuse to take no for an answer when it comes to gaining access to decisions, information and resources.

5.3   To find out about education services it may be necessary, in the 1990s, to get in touch with individual schools and colleges, rather than with a local education department, particularly as more institutions secure grant maintained status. Information, resourcing and policy-making will not be coordinated by local education authorities and citizens will have to undertake much more leg-work to build up a picture of what is going on in their areas.

5.4   Local education authorities are weakened both by the centralization of power within the government and the DES and by the increased autonomy of individual schools. Whether or not schools and the DES will prove to be more accessible to consumers than local authorities remains to be seen.

5.5   I have tried to give you a sense of the ways in which power is distributed between the participants in the education system – who seems to be losing ground and who seems to be gaining. Significant changes in the balance of power are rare. How do you think responsibilities for education should be distributed?

6   INVESTIGATIONS

What do school governors do? What powers do they have?

6.1   Make a comparison of the expectations placed on governors with the job they actually carry out in a primary, secondary or special school. If you are a governor yourself, choose a different school. To find out the expectations on governors and their legal duties, besides referring to Figure 1, you may need to borrow the *Guide to Governors* issued to every governor by the DES.

6.2 Try to arrange to observe a governors' meeting by approaching the chair of governors, explaining the purpose and assuring him or her of confidentiality of the information between yourself and your tutor.

6.3 Arrange to talk to two or three governors and the headteacher (who may also be a governor). Select from people appointed to the governors in a variety of capacities (LEA appointee, parent, teacher, co-opted from the 'community') and involved in a variety of sub-committees (curriculum, discipline, finance, 'special needs'). In making your choice, use your experience of the governors' meeting to select people who, in sum, will provide an accurate picture of what is going on.

6.4 You might use the following questions to guide your interview, though you will wish to vary them depending on the nature of the school:

(a) What were your expectations of being a governor? How has it turned out in practice?

(b) If you were a school governor before the implementation of the Education Reform Act of 1988, what strikes you as the main changes in the role of governor? What seem to you to be the advantages and disadvantages of the role of school governing bodies under local management of schools?

(c) Do you see yourself as a delegate, acting on behalf of a particular group and voicing a collective opinion, or do you see yourself as a representative who acts as an individual?

(d) What range of tasks does your governing body undertake?

(e) Do you feel competent to participate fully in all the discussions and decision-making?

(f) What do you see as the community of your school and how far do you think that the governing body acts in that community's interests? If it does not, what gets in the way?

(g) What kind of ongoing contacts exist between the governors and the staff and pupils of the school?

(h) How far have you participated in the following activities?

- implementing the National Curriculum
- appraising members of staff
- rewarding members of staff in terms of additional allowances
- hiring and firing members of staff
- consulting with the headteacher and others on a regular basis about the work and life of the school.

'Beauty and the Beast'

6.5 Choose an advertisement for a charity that you have seen recently, preferably one which is accessible enough for you to examine several times. Perhaps you can obtain a copy for yourself.

6.6 Describe the visual imagery and the caption(s) and make a note of your initial reaction. What seems to you to be the message that the charity wishes to convey? Is this in fact the message you receive as you look at the advertisement yourself?

6.7 Canvass the opinions of up to five people whose views you might expect to be very different. If feasible, include members of the client group. Ask them about:

- the message they receive from looking at the advertisement and how they respond to it
- whose interests the advertisement serves.

6.8 Would revisions need to be made to the advertisement so that the interests of the charity's clients can be promoted?

Independent living

6.9 Consider what 'independence' means and why it is such a recurrent theme in discussions of how to meet the learning or living needs of disabled people.

6.10 Find out what range of provision for disabled adults and people with learning difficulties exists in your area. Try to arrange to observe care in the community in action and talk to service providers, support workers and their clients about the advantages and disadvantages of non-institutional care.

6.11 Consider what kind of system would best confirm people in their membership of a local community.

REFERENCES

BARNES, C. (1991) *Disabled People in Britain and Discrimination: a case for anti-discrimination legislation*, London, Huror and Co in association with the British Council of Organizations of Disabled People (BCODP).

BARNES, C. (1992) 'Civil rights and wrongs', *Guardian*, 11 March 1992, p. 25.

BATES, S. (1992) 'Scourge of the schools lobby denies rewrite of reports', *Guardian*, 15 January 1992, p. 3.

BECKETT, F. (1992) 'Stuck on a spiral staircase', *Education Guardian*, 4 February 1992, p. 23.

BLACK, J. and LAWS, S. (1986) *Living with Sickle Cell Disease*, produced for the East London Branch of the Sickle Cell Society, funded by the London Borough of Newham Race Relations Unit.

CABINET OFFICE (1991) *The Citizen's Charter: raising the standard*, London, HMSO (Cmd 1599).

DEEM, R. (1991) 'The reform of school-governing bodies: the power of the consumer over the producer?', in FLUDE, M. and HAMMER, M. (eds) *The Education Reform Act 1988*, Lewes, Falmer Press, pp. 153–72.

DEPARTMENT OF EDUCATION AND SCIENCE (1991) *The Parent's Charter: you and your child's education*, London, DES.

DYSON, S. (ed.) (1988) *Sickle-Cell Anaemia and Thalassaemia*, report of the first community conference organized by the Leicestershire Organization for Sickle-Cell Anaemia Research, Leicestershire Thalassaemia Society, Leicestershire Health Education Department.

GLENDINNING, C. (1991) 'Losing ground: social policy and disabled people in Great Britain, 1980–1990', *Disability, Handicap and Society*, **6**(1), pp. 3–19.

HACKETT, G. (1992a) 'Scots ban parents' charter leaflet', *Times Educational Supplement*, 17 January 1992, p. 3.

HACKETT, G. (1992b) 'Drastic reform on the way', *Times Educational Supplement'*, 17 January 1992, p. 7.

HACKETT, G. (1992c) 'Private inspectors opposed', *Times Educational Supplement'*, 24 January 1992, p. 4.

HER MAJESTY'S INSPECTORATE (1990) *HMI in the 1990s: the work of HM Inspectors*, London, DES.

LABOUR PARTY (1991) *Meet the Challenge. Make the Change. Good education for all.* Final report of Labour Party Policy Review for the 1990s, London, Labour Party, 150 Walworth Road, SE17 1JT.

LIBERAL DEMOCRATS (1990) *Putting Pupils First: Liberal Democrat policies for education in the 1990s*, English Green Paper 3, Liberal Democrats in England, 4 Cowley Street, London SW1P 3NB.

MACLURE, J. S. (1979) *Educational Documents: England and Wales 1816 to the present day*, London, Methuen, 1965; paperback edition 1979.

NATIONAL CURRICULUM COUNCIL (1989a) *Implementing the National Curriculum – participation by pupils with special education needs*, York, NCC Circular Number 5, May 1989.

NATIONAL CURRICULUM COUNCIL (1989b) *A Curriculum for All – special needs in the National Curriculum*, York, NCC, September 1989.

OSWIN, M. (1978) *Children Living in Long-stay Hospitals*, London, Spastics International 'Medical' Publications Monograph 5.

SHARRON, H. (1991) 'Goodbye to all that: the Fallon interview', *Managing Schools Today*, **1** (1).

SHEARER, A. (1980) *Handicapped Children in Residential Care: a study of policy failure*, London, Bedford Square Press.

SIMON, B. (1991) *Education and the Social Order 1940–1990*, London, Lawrence and Wishart, Studies in the History of Education series.

SMITH, S. and JORDAN, A. (1991) *What the Papers Say and Don't Say about Disability*, London, The Spastics Society.

STATHAM, J. and MACKINNON, D. with CATHCART, H. and HALES, M. (1991) *The Education Fact File: a handbook of education information in the UK*, London, Hodder and Stoughton in association with the Open University, 1989; 2nd edition 1991.

TIMES EDUCATIONAL SUPPLEMENT (1991) 'Governors' power in dispute', *TES*, 1 November 1991, p. 2.

TIMES EDUCATIONAL SUPPLEMENT (1992) 'Parish pump politics', *TES* editorial comment, 17 January 1992, p. 19.

WHITBREAD, N. (1992) 'Teachers and parents as management partners', *Forum*, **34** (2), Spring 1992, pp. 36–7.

WINTOUR, P. and BATES, S. (1992) 'Lords overturn bill on school inspectors', *Guardian*, 3 March 1992, p. 22.

Acknowledgements

Grateful acknowledgement is made to the following for permission to reproduce material in this unit:

Page 14: 'Citizen's Charter' p.13, reproduced with the permission of the Controller of her Majesty's Stationery Office; *page* 28: The Spastics Society and Multiple Sclerosis Society; *page* 29: posters by David Hevey, funded by the Joseph Rowntree Trust.

E242: UNIT TITLES

Unit 1/2   Making Connections

Unit 3/4   Learning from Experience

Unit 5   Right from the Start

Unit 6/7   Classroom Diversity

Unit 8/9   Difference and Distinction

Unit 10   Reading Critically

Unit 11/12   Happy Memories

Unit 13   Further and Higher

Unit 14   Power in the System

Unit 15   Local Authority?

Unit 16   Learning for All